What does it mean to have
Dyslexia

D0414490

Louise Spilsbury

Heinemann LIBRARY

www.heinemann.co.uk/library
Visit our website to find out more information about Heinemann Library books.

To order:
☎ Phone 44 (0) 1865 888066
🖹 Send a fax to 44 (0) 1865 314091
🖥 Visit the Heinemann Bookshop at www.heinemann.co.uk/library to browse our catalogue and order online.

First published in Great Britain by Heinemann Library,
Halley Court, Jordan Hill, Oxford OX2 8EJ,
a division of Reed Educational and Professional Publishing Ltd.
Heinemann is a registered trademark of Reed Educational and Professional Publishing Ltd.

OXFORD MELBOURNE AUCKLAND
JOHANNESBURG BLANTYRE GABORONE
IBADAN PORTSMOUTH (NH) USA CHICAGO

Designed by AMR
Illustrated by David Woodroffe
Originated by Dot Gradations
Printed in China by Wing King Tong

ISBN 0 431 13936 9 (hardback)   ISBN 0 431 13943 1 (paperback)
05 04 03   06 05 04 03
10 9 8 7 6 5 4 3 2   10 9 8 7 6 5 4 3 2 1

British Library Cataloguing in Publication Data
Spilsbury, Louise
    What does it mean to have dyslexia?
    1.Dyslexia – Juvenile literature
    I.Title II.Dyslexia
    616.8'553

Acknowledgements
The publishers would like to thank the following for permission to reproduce photographs: Corbis: pp.7, 10, 17, 23, 27; John Walmsley: pp.4, 15, 24, 25, 26; Last Resort: p. 16; Sally and Richard Greenhill: pp.6, 9, 11, 14, 22; Trevor Clifford: pp.5, 12, 13, 18, 19, 20, 21, 28, 29.

The pictures on the following pages were posed by models who do not have dyslexia: pp.5, 6, 7, 9, 10, 11, 12, 13, 14, 15, 16, 17, 18, 19, 24, 25, 26, 27.

Special thanks to: Paul and Anthony.

The publishers would also like to thank: Judy Schiller, Oxford Dyslexia Association, and Julie Johnson, PHSE Consultant Trainer and Writer, for their help in the preparation of this book.

Cover photograph reproduced with permission of Trevor Clifford.

Every effort has been made to contact copyright holders of any material reproduced in this book.
Any omissions will be rectified in subsequent printings if notice is given to the publishers.

Contents

What is dyslexia?   4

What causes dyslexia?   6

What is dyslexia like?   8

Identifying dyslexia   10

Meet Richard   12

Dealing with dyslexia   14

Ways of learning   16

Reading and writing   18

Meet Paul   20

Living with dyslexia   22

At school   24

At home   26

Meet Anthony   28

Glossary   30

Helpful books and addresses   31

Index   32

Any words appearing in the text in bold, **like this**, are explained in the Glossary.

What is dyslexia?

The word 'dyslexia' means 'difficulty with words'. If there are children in your school who have dyslexia, it simply means they have certain difficulties with reading, writing and spelling. They may also have trouble reading numbers or notes on a sheet of music. Some dyslexics also find it hard to concentrate or remember things.

Dyslexic difficulties

These are some of the problems children with dyslexia have. You may do some of these things yourself. This in itself does not mean you have dyslexia.

- Leaving letters out – reading 'tie' instead of 'time'.
- Reading 'a' instead of 'and', or 'from' instead of 'for'.
- Swapping letters – reading 'hostipal' instead of 'hospital'.
- Putting letters the wrong way up – reading 'u' for 'n', or 'm' for 'w'.
- Mirror writing or reading letters – writing 'b' instead of 'd', or reading 'was' for 'saw'.
- Adding letters to words – 'thin' instead of 'tin'.

If you are dyslexic, it can be hard to make sense of the symbols – words, letters, numbers or notes – on a piece of paper.

People with dyslexia have a great many things they are talented at and enjoy doing very much.

How we learn

We learn about the world in a whole range of different ways. We learn by doing and using things. We learn from other people – by copying, watching or talking to them. We gain a lot of information from the experiences we have and the programmes we watch on television. Lots of people get much of their knowledge and understanding through reading.

Learning through reading – literacy – is the kind that is hard for dyslexics. All of us have things we are good at and those we are not good at. The difference is that if you are not very good at music or sport, you can get away with it. No one considers it to be a real problem. Literacy, on the other hand, is a part of almost every aspect of our daily lives. A vast amount of the information around us is in words – signs, labels, instructions and almost all your schoolwork. It is the importance of the written word in our lives that turns dyslexia into a difficulty rather than just a difference.

What causes dyslexia?

No one knows for certain what causes dyslexia, this 'difficulty with words'. Scientists do know that it is something to do with the way the **brain** works. They have studied pictures of different brains, taken with very high-tech equipment. These show that when people with dyslexia read, the parts of the brain used for language are less active than those of other people.

Scientists have found that the pathways which pass messages around the brain are arranged differently in people with dyslexia. This means that sometimes messages about what has been heard or read get muddled up. Their eyes and ears often work a little differently, too. This means that the words they see on a page often look a bit different from how other people see them. They hear sounds differently from other people. It often works the other way round, too. Some people with dyslexia struggle to find the words to express what they want to say.

Some children with dyslexia find that when a teacher asks them a question they just cannot get the right words out, even though they know the answer.

6

Who gets it?

Doctors have discovered that dyslexia is a **genetic condition**. This means that it is passed from parent to child. It is something that a child is born with. Children **inherit** a lot of different characteristics from their parents, from hair or eye colour to the shape of features like ears and noses. This is why people in the same family often look like one another. If someone in your family has dyslexia, there is a greater chance that you might have dyslexia as well.

Facts about dyslexia

- Dyslexia is the most common cause of reading, writing and spelling difficulties.
- Dyslexia is something you are born with. It is a part of who you are and you will have it all your life.
- About one in ten people have some kind of dyslexia.
- About four out of every ten people who have dyslexia have quite serious difficulties and may need special help.

Anyone can be born with dyslexia, but it tends to run in families.

What is dyslexia like?

There is no simple way of explaining exactly what dyslexia is like. This is mainly because it differs from person to person. People can be affected in many different ways. For example, some children with dyslexia can hardly read at all, whereas others just find that they have difficulty with spelling.

Many people with dyslexia find reading and writing difficult because they cannot learn and remember the way different symbols – letters, words and numbers – look. This affects the way they see words on a page. If you cannot make a picture in your head of letters or numbers, it is hard to remember what they look like or which ones to use. The words may look fuzzy or blurry, or they may appear muddled up or back to front. The three pictures on this page show you how words on a page can look to some people with dyslexia. Can you imagine learning to read if the words looked like this?

Whe nso mepeop lelook ata page thew ord
sare n otsp aced cor rect ly.
Somepeoplewhohavedyslexiaseewordsall
crushedtogetherwhentheytrytoread.

Some people who have dyslexia say that the words on a page look shadowed or doubled when they try to read.
Some people who have dyslexia say that the words on a page look shadowed or doubled when they try to read.

Some people with dyslexia say that the words on a page look blurred from a central point when they try to read them.
Some people with dyslexia say that the words on a page look blurred from a central point when they try to read them.

Memory

One of the reasons people with dyslexia have difficulties with reading and writing is that they find it hard to remember things, such as how to spell a word. This means they may find it hard to remember things they have just been told, like a set of directions or instructions. They may also have trouble with telling the time or with putting things in order, such as days of the week or months of the year, or learning times tables.

Special skills

On the positive side, dyslexia often gives people special talents and strengths. Many children who have dyslexia are very imaginative and make up wonderful stories. They may be good at drama (acting) and music, or with computers. Others excel at sport. Some find that they are really good with their hands and able to mend things quite easily. Others know how to make things look good, whether designing a page for a school magazine or arranging the school hall for a concert.

Identifying dyslexia

Dyslexia can be hard to identify. Most children make mistakes in spelling and reading that are similar to those made by children with dyslexia. Even special doctors who know a lot about dyslexia can take a long time to decide whether someone has dyslexia. It is important to identify dyslexia as early as possible, though, because it is much easier for people with dyslexia to learn if they get some extra help when they are young.

First signs

There are signs which can indicate dyslexia long before a child learns to read and write, when he or she is a **toddler**. These include a child taking a little longer than usual to learn to walk or to speak clearly. They may jumble up their words or be slow to learn nursery rhymes or the names for colours. They may have trouble remembering the correct names for objects, such as 'table' and 'chair'. On the other hand, they may be gifted in other ways, such as being able to build wonderful models and paint lovely pictures.

Some young children with dyslexia have trouble remembering what order to do things in, for example, when tying laces.

Once children who have dyslexia know what is causing their difficulties, they often feel much happier.

Finding out – assessment

Most children who have dyslexia find out they have trouble with reading or writing when they start school. At first they may have eye and ear tests to check if their difficulties are caused by sight or hearing problems. Once these have been ruled out, they may meet with a **specialist** who knows about the different ways people learn.

The child completes a range of tests with the specialist. This is called an **assessment**. One of the tests works out how clever they are – dyslexics are usually as clever and sometimes cleverer than most people. This may not show up at school because of the difficulties they have with reading and writing. The tests also find out how they organize their work and thoughts. Their reading, writing and spelling, mathematical and memory abilities are also tested. If the specialist is certain they have dyslexia, they work out what kind of help they need.

Meet Richard

My name is Richard. I'm nine now but I found out I have dyslexia two years ago, when I was seven. Until I was seven, I loved school. Mum says I was always ready to rush out the door long before it was really time for school to start. Then I started to have trouble at school. I just couldn't do the work. The teacher always seemed to be telling me off and people in my class called me names.

I was having trouble with reading mostly. Sometimes I'd leave whole words or sentences out and it took me ages to write anything. The teacher was always making me redo work because it was too messy and smudged. I hardly ever got a break time because I was redoing work or I had to stay in to finish copying things off the board. I got really angry when people teased me and sometimes I just hit out. I couldn't help it. I just got so fed up. That just got me into even more trouble, of course. It got so I'd be crying every day before school and pretending I had a headache or stomach-ache so I could stay at home.

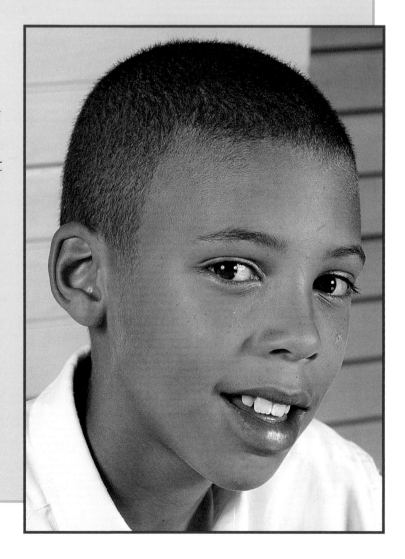

At first I think Mum and Dad thought I was just being silly. Then one day Mum read a magazine article while she was waiting in the dentist's. It was about dyslexia. I'd been saying things like 'I'm no good' and 'I'm stupid' and she realized I might have dyslexia. She talked to my teacher the very next day. After my **assessment**, the school sorted out some extra help for me.

Alex comes in twice a week to help me out. He's so cool that no one teases me about having extra help. I'm doing much better at school now. My reading and writing are improving all the time. I wrote this on a computer that has a spell checker, so that helps! Mum reads things through for me, too. I feel so much happier now that I know it's not just me being stupid. In fact my teacher says I'm doing really well and Mum and Dad are going to be really proud when they see my school report!

Dealing with dyslexia

Before you know you have dyslexia, life can be tough. It may feel as if no one understands you and teachers are always telling you off. Some people complain that you don't pay attention or teachers tell you to try harder. They get cross because they don't understand why you never seem to finish work in time. You may start to believe you are not very clever. You may feel embarrassed that you cannot write very well and try to hide it.

Most young people with dyslexia find that with help they can catch up and get on with achieving what they are truly capable of.

Some people say it is a relief when they find out they are dyslexic. It explains why they have been feeling confused and unable to get on with their work. They are glad to know that other people understand and that there are ways teachers and others can help them. For many, just knowing that their problems have nothing to do with being less clever than everyone else can make them feel a lot better about themselves.

Help at school

The kind of teaching help you need if you are dyslexic depends on the kinds of difficulties you have and what suits you best. Some people, especially those who are very dyslexic, go to special schools. Here, children are taught in smaller groups, say between six and eight pupils, all the time. All their teachers have had training and experience in teaching people with dyslexia.

Most children with dyslexia go to ordinary schools, where they work alongside everyone else. Some may have a helper to work beside them in the classroom. They may also work alone or in a small group with another teacher for a couple of hours a week. This gives them the chance to work at their own pace and time to think things through. They can perhaps ask for questions to be answered or problems to be explained in a way they can understand more easily.

If you are dyslexic, working one-to-one with a special teacher gives you time to work through different ways of learning to read or spell, at your own pace.

Ways of learning

Young people with dyslexia can learn as well as anyone else. The only difference is that they may need to learn some things in different ways. Some dyslexics find it easier to remember letters and words if they meet them in many different forms.

As well as reading the words, they say them, hear them, and perhaps touch and see them in different ways, all at the same time. For example, some children touch and look at wooden letters as they say and hear them. Others may make the letters in a special way, for example in clay or even by writing them in the air.

Some dyslexics find it easier to learn their alphabet if they can see and touch the letters, as well as say the sounds they make.

Using your eyes, ears, voice and hands all at the same time like this means that your **brain** gets the same information from all these senses at once. You have a memory of the way the letters look and feel, as well as the way they sound. This helps you take in the information in such a way that it should be easier to remember next time you meet the letters.

Using computers

Many dyslexics are very good at using computers, which can help them in different ways. If you have trouble spelling or writing, it can help to key in (or type up) schoolwork on a computer. It is easy to correct your work using spelling and **grammar** checking programmes.

Some children with dyslexia find that it helps to use a talking computer. By wearing earphones and using a **microphone**, children with dyslexia can speak directly to a computer. The computer recognizes the words and types them up. That way you do not have to worry about spelling words or forming letter shapes. Some computers read back the words you have spoken so you can check what you have written. The computer reads one word at a time. This is helpful if you are dyslexic because it helps you to slow down and order your thoughts before putting them on paper.

It can take quite a long time to train a computer to recognize your voice, but it is often worth the trouble. If you have difficulty writing what you want to say on paper, **voice recognition computers** can do it for you.

Reading and writing

When most people learn to read, they see a word and connect the way it looks with what it means. This can be hard for people with dyslexia. They may have trouble remembering the links between the way words look and what they mean, or the words may look jumbled up on the page. Some people who have dyslexia say they tend to think in pictures. They may find it easier to learn words that describe something you can see, such as a ruler or a textbook. It is harder for them to learn words that don't link to objects, such as 'was', 'happy', 'nothing' or 'though'.

It may help to learn just a few words at a time. This gives you a chance to use and recall those words, before moving on to new ones. Sometimes children with dyslexia create their own dictionary or word bank to record and practise any new or difficult words they meet. They can also jot down anything which they know will help them remember what the words mean and how they sound.

Recording new words you meet in your own dictionary is a great way of expanding your vocabulary.

One of the problems people with dyslexia have is expressing themselves through writing. It can be frustrating to have lots of ideas, but be unable to get them down on paper. Some dyslexics learn joined-up handwriting as early as possible. Joining letters together can help to remind you of their order in a particular word. It also helps to learn **grammar** (the rules of language), such as spelling patterns, letters that always go together ('igh') and those that never go together ('ihg'). With the right help, people with dyslexia can learn to read and write perfectly well.

Talking books

Many people enjoy listening to '**talking books**' – stories read by an actor or even the author and recorded onto cassette tapes. You can buy them in shops or borrow them from libraries. They are fun to listen to, especially on long car journeys or at bedtime. They are useful if you are dyslexic as you can listen to books you might find difficult to read by yourself. Some people like to read from a copy of the book as they listen.

Meet Paul

I'm Paul. I'm twelve years old and I go to secondary school. The thing I like best is sport. At school I play for the football, cricket and rugby teams. This season we played football matches against other schools and we won all our matches, except one. I like any sport, really, especially golf. At weekends and in the evenings I like riding my bike and playing football with my friend Matthew. We play on the field which is just at the bottom of my garden. I like listening to music as well. I like some pop music, especially rap and some singers, like Gabrielle.

I also play on my computer a lot. I play games on it and I do times tables and English on it to help me with my schoolwork. I like school but some of the work is hard. That is because I've got dyslexia. Dyslexia is when it's hard to spell and read and you work more slowly than other people sometimes.

Most of the time when I'm at school I have lessons with everyone else in my class. I have two support lessons at school and an extra one at the weekend. At school I have a teacher called Mrs Chaplin. She takes me into the reference library and does some work with me. We do spelling, reading, crosswords, word puzzles and other games to help me with my spelling and reading. One of the puzzles we do is Word Search, when you have to find words in a box full of letters. I have one lesson with Mrs Chaplin on Mondays while the rest of the class do Religious Studies, and one on Wednesdays instead of assembly.

On Saturday mornings I do spellings and stuff with some other kids with a teacher called Mrs Martin. I don't always feel like doing it, but I know it's going to help me. After school I have to do about 30 minutes' homework every day, though it's sometimes less. Sometimes Mum or Dad helps me a bit, but mostly I do it on my own.

Living with dyslexia

Have you ever heard the saying 'Sticks and stones may break my bones, but names will never hurt me'? It isn't true, is it? We all know that being called names can hurt your feelings, sometimes badly. Some people who have dyslexia find that they are teased or picked on by others. They may be called lazy or stupid, or people may say things like: 'There's no such thing as dyslexia. It's just an excuse for being stupid.' The fact is that people who say things like this are showing their own ignorance, no one else's. If you are dyslexic, you are as clever as anyone else, and you probably work twice as hard as other people. You also have to be very determined and strong-willed to keep on with work that at times may seem impossible. You may have extra teaching at weekends or in the evenings. This takes a lot of self-discipline.

Some people feel better if their teacher explains to their class what dyslexia is and why they need extra support sometimes.

There are times when most people who have dyslexia would prefer not to have to deal with the difficulties it can cause. It can be frustrating to feel as if you are behind other people in your class, or when younger brothers or sisters become better at reading than you are. We all have moments when we feel like this about things we have problems with. At such times it can help to focus on the things you are good at.

Many people like the fact that having dyslexia gives them a special slant on life. They say that it gives them the ability to see the 'bigger picture', to see things from a different angle to other people. This can help you achieve success in many different careers, such as art, **architecture**, design, drama, electronics, **engineering**, mechanics, music and computers. Many famous people are dyslexic, from great thinkers, like Albert Einstein, to business **entrepreneurs**, like Richard Branson, and actors, like Tom Cruise.

Richard Branson had difficulties at school because of his dyslexia, but went on to become one of the world's most famous and successful businessmen.

At school

If you have dyslexia there are lots of ways you can work around any difficulties you meet in the school day. You may not need to do any of these things, or you may find that all of them help.

- Ask your teacher to leave information up on a blackboard or overhead projector. You may need more time to copy it, especially if there are some tricky words in there.
- Use a tape recorder to record lessons and make notes for yourself from the tape later on.
- Ask your teacher to check you have understood or written down tasks correctly. It might help if they underline any important points or questions, too.
- Sit at the front of the class for subjects you have trouble with. It is easier to concentrate if people are not in your way and you can easily ask the teacher to explain things again, if needs be.
- Speak up in discussion groups when you can. If you have trouble writing things down, this is a great chance to show what you know.

If you think you have missed something, you could always ask to borrow a friend's notes to copy.

Don't forget that school is not just about learning how to read and write. It's also a chance to find other things you are good at, like music and sport, and to meet different people.

Cartoon capers!

Many people who have dyslexia are very good at drawing. Some say that they even think in pictures, not words. This means that although they have some great story ideas, they may not be able to write them down on paper. Some teachers allow students with dyslexia to write their stories in cartoon form. Labels or **speech bubbles** help to tell the story and, as these are usually short, they are not as hard to write as pages of text.

Testing times

It helps children with dyslexia to have extra time to do an exam or test. They may need, say, an extra fifteen minutes for every hour that is usually allowed. This gives them the same chance to do well in a test as other children in their class. In important exams some people who have serious difficulties are allowed to have a teacher read out the questions to them and also write down their answers for them.

At home

Home is where we go at the end of the day to rest, have fun and unwind. The free time we have in the evenings and weekends is also our chance to enjoy our hobbies, whether at home or somewhere else. This is important if you are dyslexic. If you are having difficulties with schoolwork, it is good to spend time doing things you like or are especially good at. Try new things when you can. You never know what else you might be good at, from model-making to mountain-biking – and one of these things might turn into a great job when you are grown up!

You never know what you might be good at unless you give it a try!

Homework hints

If you are dyslexic, you may have trouble remembering things like homework. It might help to write lists and timetables. Keep these at home to remind you what you need each day and when you should do your homework. It may help to add pictures so you can see at a glance what you need to do. This is good advice for everyone – most of us would benefit from being better organized!

Enjoying stories

Some people who have dyslexia say they never enjoy reading stories. This is often because many of the books aimed at children their age are too hard for them to read, and books they can read are meant for younger children, which they usually find boring or silly. There are many books around today that are gripping stories on all kinds of topics, from football to fantasy, written in a simple and direct style. Books with pictures or cartoons can help if you find it hard to remember complicated plots or too many different characters in storylines.

Don't forget, though, that reading is not the only way to enjoy a good story. As well as **talking books** (stories on tapes or CDs), there are lots of other ways of enjoying stories. You can watch films on television or experience the excitement of a live performance of a play at the theatre.

If you have trouble reading, it does not mean you cannot enjoy a good story. If you keep searching you may find an author or style of book that you like.

Meet Anthony

Hi. My name's Anthony and I'm twelve years old. I have dyslexia but I think it's only a problem if you see it as one. If you imagine you haven't got it you can just get on with things. I try to make it the smallest problem. For me all it does is make me spell things wrong, so it's writing stuff down I have trouble with. I don't have extra help at school. But on Saturday mornings I go with some friends for extra tuition (teaching). There are two people to a teacher. That helps quite a bit. The teachers make the work challenging but not too hard. We get to plan half a lesson each. I wanted to do a report on my last school week. Sometimes I do cartoons to tell the story, like in a comic.

I've got a talking computer. I talk and it writes the words down. If you say a word wrong it says it back to you so you know it's wrong and you can delete it and go back and say it right. I'll be able to do my homework on it. I can type quite well.

At school I particularly like maths and science. I like science because you get to do lots of experiments. I play for a football team. We train Friday nights and play on Sunday afternoons. I'm quite good at BMX-ing and I like skiing, too.

I'm part of a group called Young **Engineers**. We all have dyslexia and we get together to do some brilliant stuff. We have an absolutely fabulous organizer who helped us enter a competition to design the best electric car. It looks like a Formula 1 car. It's about 2.5–3 metres long and it runs on batteries. We designed it and built it and we even designed our own boiler suits. One of the boys in the group, his dad owns a garage and we did it there. We raced it in a competition and we did really well. We came seventh out of more than 30 other cars. Now I'm organizing a day out to a dry ski slope for the group. You fall over but it doesn't really hurt. It's brilliant.

Glossary

architecture design or construction of buildings

assessment to find out whether or not someone has dyslexia, they have an assessment. This usually involves doing some tests and talking to a specialist who knows a lot about dyslexia.

brain organ inside your skull. It is the control centre of the body, telling the rest of your body what to do and dealing with thoughts, ideas, feelings and memories.

condition word used to describe an illness or disease that a person has for a long time, perhaps all their life. It is also often used to describe an illness that a person is born with.

engineer someone who designs or builds machines or structures such as bridges

engineering designing or building machines, or structures such as bridges

entrepreneur person who runs a business or company and risks making or losing money. Successful entrepreneurs often create many jobs for other people in their business.

genetic to do with your genes. Genes are substances within the father's sperm and the mother's eggs that determine what a baby is like. They are also present in all body cells acting to control these cells.

grammar rules about how you use words together. For example, you should always say 'I am', not 'I is'.

inherit an inherited condition is one that is passed from parents to their children

microphone piece of equipment that collects sounds and sends them out from a speaker

specialist someone who has a lot of training and experience in a particular subject. Specialists in dyslexia know all about the condition and understand its complicated symptoms.

speech bubbles circles coming from a character's mouth in cartoons in books or comics with words to show what they are saying

talking books stories read by an actor or author and recorded onto cassette tapes or CDs

toddler young child. Toddlers are so-called because they may not be old enough to walk properly, so they 'toddle'.

voice recognition computers computers that can be taught to recognize your voice and write down the words you say, so you don't need to key or type them in

Helpful books and addresses

BOOKS

Barrington Stoke series: Enjoyable stories written by well-known authors for children who have difficulties with reading. Available through Heinemann Library.

Let's Discuss Dyslexia and Associated Difficulties, Pete Sanders and Steve Myers, Franklin Watts, 1996

The Ace Spelling Dictionary: Find Words Quickly and Improve Your Spelling, David Moseley, Learning Development Aids, 1995

Stiks and Stoans, Andrew Matthews, Mammoth, 1999

Moving the Goalposts, Rob Childs, A&C Black, 1998

WEBSITES

www.kidshealth.org/parent/medical/learning/dyslexia

www.interdys.org/abcsofdyslexia/page-infobasic.asp

www.discoveryschool.com/dyslexia

ORGANIZATIONS

British Dyslexia Association
98 London Road
Reading RG1 5AU
Tel: 0118 966 2677
Fax: 0118 935 1927
E-mail: info@dyslexiahelp-bda.demon.co.uk
Website: www.bda-dyslexia.org.uk

Dyslexia Institute
133 Gresham Road
Staines
Middlesex TW18 2AJ
Tel: 01784 463851
Fax: 01784 460747
Website: www.dyslexia-inst.org.uk

Arts Dyslexia Trust
Executive Secretary
Lodge Cottage
Brabourne Lees
Ashford
Kent TN25 6QZ
Tel/Fax: 01303 813221
E-mail: sp.artsdysx@demon.co.uk

IN AUSTRALIA

Specific Learning Difficulties Association of South Australia (SPELD)
298 Portrush Road
Kensington, SA 5068
Australia
Tel: 08 8431 1655
Fax: 08 8364 5751
E-mail: info@speld-sa.org.au
Website: www.speld-sa.org.au

Dyslexia Information Service
213 Fullarton Road
Eastwood SA 5063
Australia
Tel: 08 8373 7020
Fax: 08 8373 7018

Index

assessment 11, 13

brain 6, 16

causes of dyslexia 6
computers 13, 17, 20, 28
concentration 4
coping with dyslexia 14–15, 24–5
creativity 9, 10

dictionaries and word banks 18
drawing 25
dyslexic difficulties 4

exams and tests 25

family history 7
first signs of dyslexia 10

genetic condition 7
grammar 19

hobbies and interests 20, 26, 29
home life 26–7
homework 26

identifying dyslexia 10–11

learning process 5, 16–17
literacy 5
living with dyslexia 22–3

mathematical abilities 11
memory 4, 9, 11
mirror writing 4
music 4

people affected by dyslexia 7

reading and writing 4, 5, 7, 8, 10, 11, 12, 18–19, 27

school and schoolwork 12, 15, 20–1, 24–5, 29
special schools 15
special talents 9, 10, 23
specialist teachers 13, 15, 21, 28
spelling 4, 7, 8, 10, 11, 19
spelling and grammar checkers 13, 17

talking books 19, 27
teasing 12, 22
testing for dyslexia 11

voice recognition computers 17, 28

words on a page, appearance of 8